Youth
Asks,
What's Life For

YOUTH FORUM SERIES

Titles in Print

YOUTH FORUM SERIES

Youth
Asks,

WHAT'S LIFE FOR

That They May See

by
D. T. Niles

THOMAS NELSON & SONS
London   Camden, N.J.   Toronto

Library of Congress Catalog Card Number: 68-22130
design by Harold Leach

Printed in the United States of America

Foreword

Written in the context of the Christian faith, this book is one in a series published by Thomas Nelson & Sons in collaboration with Church Youth Research.

The research agency, which serves as editor of this series, is known through *What Youth Are Thinking* (Smedsrud, 1961) and *Profiles of Church Youth* (Strommen, 1963). The Director, Dr. Merton Strommen, is known also for his work as Director of Research (1965-67) with Religious Education Association, an inter-faith agency serving all church groups.

The purpose of the series is to use points of established need to bring about meaningful contact between the GOSPEL of God in Jesus Christ and YOUNG PEOPLE. Underlying the total effort is a concern that youth throughout the English-speaking world can be helped to see that the Gospel of Christ is the core of life itself in all its realities.

Unique to this publication effort is the use that is made of research findings. These describe the specific need to which each book is addressed as well as the youth most concerned about this need. Thus a writer is helped to speak more directly to the actual conflicts, values, and beliefs of an important segment of youth.

The significance of this series is enhanced by the scholarship and pastoral concern of the authors. Their grasp of the fields in which each writes enables them to speak with authority, establishing the series as a basic reference in the area of youth work.

To
Damayanthi

Introduction

A sixty-year-old man has written a provocative book for young people.

In our day, that's news!

His name is Daniel Thamyrajan Niles. He's a clergyman. He lives in Ceylon. You have the book in your hands.

Youth Asks, What's Life For is not a jazzy book. It's a solid one. Dr. Niles assumes youth are not half as interested in what adults think youth ought to know as they are in what adults really think. The book tells what He thinks . . . and what He believes.

Of course, this is an adult evaluation, but look at these knife-like excerpts:

Jesus Christ is not available for casual acquaintance.
To believe is to turn towards and to remain face to face.
Forgiveness is past tense.
All choices have to be paid for.
There is no cure for second-hand doubt.
The devil allows credit but God demands payment in advance.
Christ is the Master of every situation, including death.
We must live close enough to people so they can see us as we really are.

Dr. Niles is a good writer, with more than a dozen titles to his credit. He communicates simply and conversationally. It's easy reading.

But *What's Life For* is more than style. It's Dr. Niles himself. He is pastoral, Biblical, personal and evangelical. When things like these are for real, the message is bound to come through. And we're bound to listen.

Thankfully the book reflects the spirit and voice of the younger churches. The word "young," I hope you agree, means youthful and fresh rather than inexperienced or immature. *What's Life For* is an unvarnished approach built on the conviction that the fresh air of Heaven is still plainly blowing. Or, to borrow another phrase from J. B. Phillips, it's evidence of "the young church in action!"

More than anything else, the book is worthwhile because of the issues it tackles. "To turn around is not enough." Dr. Niles leads his readers face to face with God. It is not so much that one places faith on Christ, as that one is placed on Christ. The notion of believing is so radical that it *must* be compared to new birth, to death, to resurrection. To be forgiven by God in Christ is not simply to be rid of one's guilt. It is to enter into the forgiving activity of God.

"Jesus Christ is *not* available for casual acquaintance. Eventually it is a choice for or against Christ," says Dr. Niles, "not a choice between Him and someone else." He writes so *that they may see* that to be a Christian is to be committed to God in Jesus Christ, to belong to the Christian community, and to live the life of a servant.

In less able hands, this Christian Witnessing theme could have deteriorated into an easy-to-use manual on evangelism. Dr. Niles sees through and beyond this. He knows "life is rooted in choice and is constantly carried forward by choices." He recognizes the Kingdom of God comes crashing into our lives and into the life of the world. He sees that God's rule over all things has become visible and tangible in the Christ-event.

> There is a place in Christian witness for talking about Jesus; there is an equal place for not talking about Him, for just getting on with the job in hand."

That's what the book is about.
And I am glad!

Epiphany, 1968

Elmer N. Witt
Chicago, Illinois

Contents

That they may see

This little book is one in a series, and its title in the series is, YOUTH ASKS, WHAT'S LIFE FOR. But, as a book with its own individuality, it has another title "That they may see."

After Jesus fed the five thousand, and returned to the western shore of the lake of Galilee, crowds followed Him. Jesus said to them, "You seek me because you ate and were filled and not because you saw the sign which I performed." (John 6:26). They could have answered, "Of course, we saw what you did. You fed five thousand people with five loaves and two fish." Still Jesus was right in saying that they did not see. They saw neither that it was the Father in heaven who fed them, nor that Jesus was the bread from heaven by which men were nourished.

When the Holy Spirit came on the disciples on the day of Pentecost and they spoke in other tongues as the Spirit gave them utterance, some of the bystanders explained what had happened by saying that they were drunk. (Acts 2:1-4). When Paul made his defence before Festus, Festus was content to say, "Paul, you are mad." (Acts 26:24).

It is not always easy to see. And sometimes, where one sees another does not. When John and Peter were interviewed by the Sanhedrin, their answers made many say, "Their behavior has no explanation except that these men have been with Jesus." (Acts 4:13)

What do men see when they see us? The gospel writer says that those who saw Jesus recognized in Him the Son of the Father full of grace and truth. (John 1:14). Is it not often the case that those who see us, see in us only the behaviour of insecure orphans in a homeless world? We give no impression of being children of the Father.

Jesus said, "Let your light so shine before men, that they may see your good works and give glory to your Father who is in heaven." (Matt. 5:16). The problem of Christian witness is to help men see into and beyond the life which God enables us to live, so that they may discern how glorious is the Father to whose work we testify. They must so see that they are led to speak about God and not about us. They must so see that they recognize the meaning of our lives as lying in heaven and not on earth. They must so see that they discover themselves as belonging with us in the family of a common Father.

But if this is to happen, a light must be shed on our lives and our living: light by that flame which Jesus Christ has kindled in us and by which alone the actual lights and shadows of our lives can be explained. Not even our goodness can by itself point to God.

Also, this hope and prayer that others will see Jesus Christ through us has to be grounded in our own ability to see others in Him. That some of them do not believe in Him, or do not know Him, is no hindrance to our remembering that they too belong to Him, because He has already died for them. A Christian witness has constantly to wrestle with the question, "How do I see someone else in Jesus Christ?" On this vision will depend the validity of the ways in which we shall seek to lead them to Him.

Jesus said, "I, when I am lifted up from the earth, will draw all men to myself." (John 12:32). Our task, both as individuals and as a community, is to lift Him up by word and deed: rather, to show Him who was lifted up by a way of life and a form of speech which are appropriate for such a testimony. It is He who draws. In other words, our lives are but a pointing finger, pointing away from us to Him; and pointing to Him in such a way, that those among whom we stand, do not feel our finger pointing at them.

The heart of Christian witness lies in helping people to see why we stand where we stand, and in persuading them to stand with us, looking at what we see.

"Oh could I tell, ye surely would believe it!
Oh could I only say what I have seen!
How should I tell or how can ye receive it?
How, till He bringeth you where I have been?" [1]

D. T. Niles

[1] "St. Paul," by F. W. H. Myers from *Sanctuary Booklets No. 3*, London: H. R. Allenson, Ltd.

The way of the argument

This introduction is addressed directly to the young people for whom this book is written and by whom it will be read. I have written it at the request of the publishers, who asked that I write in a series titled "The Youth Forum Series" on the subject of "Christian Witness," and that in the writing there be taken into account "the beliefs, the values and conflicts which actually motivate the thoughts and actions of those young people who are at the high school or secondary school age level."

But when I came to write, the book wrote itself. Convictions that had gathered in my mind as I have myself pondered on this subject forced themselves out and set themselves down. Normally, I would have not expected a book for young people to have taken this form, but it has. When I read the book through after it was written, I began to suspect that the unconscious conviction which has controlled it has been that young people are not usually helped by writing which is directly aimed at them. They do not want to know what older people, like us, think they ought to know. What they want to know is what we really think.

It will be seen that, in the development of the book, each chapter has become an exposition of some particular part of Scripture. When I started writing, I did not intend to do this. However, in the actual writing, this has happened. I think it was because, over the years, working with Christian young people, I have discovered that general talk carries no conviction. They are usually suspicious of advice and

14

amused by exhortation. But they are willing to listen when one is talking about the real reasons why he believes and what he believes.

It is never easy to demonstrate how and why Scripture holds authority; but that demonstration does not in any case take place when Scripture is dragged in to support an argument that rests on other grounds. What has happened in these chapters is that the argument of each chapter has been allowed to rest on the exposition of a particular Scripture.

- The first chapter entitled "The Issue" does not go anywhere. It simply seeks to put on the table, as it were, the concerns and anxieties which all people— young and old—have when they come to take seriously their responsibility as witnesses to Christ, and the inadequacies by which they are beset.
- In the second chapter entitled "The Event," the underlying intention is to show that Christian witness is not just a subject that we take up for discussion, but that it is a situation in which we are caught as a result of something which God does.
- In the third chapter entitled "The Choice," what is attempted is to look at the texture of the response by which we become and remain involved in the continuing activity of God in Christ.
- The fourth chapter entitled "The Family" is crucial to the whole argument. It seeks to show that the obligations and problems of Christian witness are simply an integral part of the opportunities, privileges, and perplexities of our common life. As long

as we speak of Christian witness simply in terms of "we" and "they," we do not rightly understand.

- The fifth chapter is entitled "The Adventure." It brings out the fact that the task of Christian witness is not something we do for Jesus Christ but with Him: so that the consequences of this task for us cannot be different from the consequences for Him.

- The sixth chapter is entitled "The Alternative." It was difficult to decide how to handle the subject of this chapter. At the end, I decided not to attempt any exposition of other religions or other ideologies or other ways of living and thinking which are considered to be alternatives to Christian faith and life. I decided rather to stand by the direct scriptural affirmation that the alternative to being for Christ is to be against Him.

- The seventh chapter entitled "The Call" emphasizes a critical truth which is often forgotten: that, in the last analysis, I myself am the only person whose salvation I can decisively affect.

- There is a postscript to this book. Since this book is primarily intended for young people, a chapter had to be included on the Christian home.

A book on Christian witness has itself to be a testimony to Jesus Christ and His ways with men. That, in some measure, this should be true of this book too has been my hope. At least it aims not only to discuss what Christian witness is and how it is to be borne, but also to make it.

The Issue

JAMES   Don't you think our pastor laid it on too thick this morning? He preaches a sermon on a Christian's responsibility to be a witness and assumes that his congregation, and especially we "young people" whom he particularly challenged, are sufficiently committed to the Christian faith and its practice to see the point of his challenge.

PETER   But surely he had a right to do what he did.

JAMES   I am not so sure. I suppose, for instance, that because I go to Church regularly, I am looked upon as one of the "Christian young people." But what does my minister know as to what kind of a person I really am?

JOAN   Jim, what do you mean? If you are thinking of the faults which any one of us is bound to have, surely that makes no difference to my calling myself a Christian or of other people thinking of us as Christians.

17

JAMES   Is that the real issue? What is the consequence of the fact that whenever I am away from my church company and among others, I am willing not only to drink but to get drunk?

PETER   Jim, you say that we are not the kind of people who should be challenged with the problems of Christian witness, because our problem is previous to this. Ours, in your opinion, is the problem of the Christian life. I would say rather that it is only as we face our responsibility for Christian witness that we see exactly how we are both weak and faithless in Christian living.

JUDY   My trouble is that when I am faced with the necessity or the opportunity to talk about Jesus, I lose my nerve. I suppose it is partly because I am such an unworthy representative of what it means to be a Christian and partly because I do not really know how to talk about Jesus Christ.

JOAN   I think you are right in saying that the question is one of learning to talk about Jesus Christ. We cannot begin with ourselves and our experience of Him. It is about Him that we must talk.

JAMES   I don't agree. There must be something which we can say about how He has dealt with us. Otherwise we may just as well shut up.

PETER   It seems to me that what others need to know is not so much what Jesus Christ has done for us as what He can do. Who is He? Our unwillingness to live by Him is no disproof of what He can do for us if only we will let Him.

JUDY   Why are we speaking about our witness to Jesus

Christ at all? Why should it be so significant that there is something which He has done for us? Surely, what is important is that it was He who did it.

JAMES But we know Him only by what He has done. Is that not so?

JOAN I was discussing this with Leela one day, and she put it to me like this. She said, "At home in India, when I returned from school in the evening, sometimes my mother was there to greet me and to give me my tea. At other times, my mother was not at home, and the tea was laid out for me on the table and the maid did for me anything I wanted. The deed itself was the same in either case, but it made a world of difference as to whether it was my mother or the maid who did it." Was she not right?

PETER I think the issue goes deeper than that. When we talk of Christian witness, we must realize that the talk itself arises out of not only who Jesus is, not only what He has done for us, but out of a situation that has been created by Him in which we and all our fellow-men are involved.

JUDY I am not quite sure what you mean, Peter, but if you mean what I think you mean, I am sure you are right. When we read the gospel story, we find that the disciples of Jesus began to talk about Him, not in any attempt to interpret His death or explain His life or even to tell others about His influence on them. What happened was that His resurrection exploded in their midst and made them witnesses. They were too happy to keep quiet.

JOAN   I suppose you mean that when we talk about being witnesses, we are talking about having become witnesses. We have become the kind of people who can see what the Lord is doing because He is alive and, therefore, are constantly speaking about it.

JAMES   My difficulty is with the resurrection itself. I don't find it difficult to believe that Jesus Christ is alive and that His influence is effective in the lives of Christian people, never mind exceptions like me. But when you talk about the resurrection, you obviously mean more than that. You are intending to convey the idea of an immediate presence in our midst which is Jesus Christ risen from the dead. I find this very difficult.

PETER   We have to face the question about the gospel testimony to the concreteness of the resurrection event. My father told me that the story of the empty tomb was the way chosen by the gospel writers to set forward their conviction about this concreteness.

JAMES   It is not the empty tomb that worries me. I heard my minister say in his sermon last Easter that he would not put it past God to have raised Jesus from the dead in just that way. My difficulty is with pointing to His immediate presence to which we must be able to point, if the resurrection story is true.

JOAN   Somehow we must find a way of talking about Jesus and ourselves at the same time.

JUDY   Is there any answer to the question which Jim

raises concerning Christ's immediate presence, except that there is an answer in the very existence of the Church? It must be more than a metaphor to talk of the Church as the Body of Christ!

JAMES   I am not so sure that you can so easily side-step the necessity of the individual's testimony to the presence of Jesus Christ.

PETER   It seems to me that the issue of Christian witness has three points of reference. There is Jesus Christ, there are ourselves who are His witnesses, and there are our friends to whom we must witness about Him.

JAMES   I know my own need of Him and, therefore, I know their need of Him too. It is not for me a question of sharing with them something I know, but of discovering with them something which is for them and me a common need.

JOAN   Our love for our friends must compel us to share with them what we know of Jesus.

PETER   Surely, it is the other way round. If we love them, the love of Jesus for them can use our love as a channel of His.

JUDY   It would be truer to say that we must be willing to let Jesus love them through us.

JAMES   But cannot concern and affection for other people exist independently of the Christian concern? Also, is it not true that unless we love people for their own sake, we shall not be able to love them for the sake of Jesus?

PETER   That is just the point. It is not possible to speak of Christian witness without seeing certain connections. The story of Jesus culminates in the resurrection. The fact of Jesus includes His active presence in our midst. Our need of Him explains the way in which He has got hold of us. Our love for others is part of our love for Him and His love for them.

JOAN   That is rather a mouthful, Peter, but I think that you have put your finger on the essentials.

JAMES   All this may be true. In fact, I think that it is true. But all the same, I have not yet found a way of giving up my taste for liquor.

JOAN   My problem is that beyond a certain point in the argument, I just get angry and impatient.

JUDY   Nor, I guess, will I find it easy to keep my nerve when the actual moment to witness comes.

JOAN   Will you excuse me while I run up to my room and bring something which I want to read to you. I just remembered it.

JUDY   Yes, please do.

JOAN   (returning) Here it is. When we were talking about the resurrection of Jesus, I remembered a passage which my mother read to me from a novel she was reading. I was so intrigued by that passage that she copied it out for me and gave it to me. Let me read it to you. You will find its relevance to what we have been talking about. It refers to a character by the name of Joseph Vance in a novel by William de Morgan.

"He was a Christian who had endeavoured to strain off the teachings of Jesus the Nazarene from the scum and dregs of the world and the Churches, and never been able to decide on the mesh of the strainer . . . He seemed always to be endeavouring to find a sieve that would let Christ through and keep the miracles out. But do what he would, the Resurrection slipped past. The stone that was rolled away from the sepulchre, broke a hole in the mesh and the Gadarene swine found it out and came through with a rush, and then a new sieve had to be provided and the whole operation repeated."

JUDY   That is a quaint way of describing our situation. But it is absolutely right. The resurrection keeps tearing holes. We never do manage to keep it out, and by that I mean we are never left to our own devices, even when we are seeking to witness to Him. I have often wondered whether our talk about Him is simply a kind of stage whisper accompanying the main drama. His activity as He seeks to win disciples is the determining reality.

PETER   I now see the meaning of something I read some time ago. The writer was saying that we do not live inside a closed world and that there was always the nearness of miracle.

JOAN   Yes, the hole made by the resurrection of Jesus is a hole in our very world. The resurrection repeats itself, and on that miracle we depend for everything.

JUDY   You mean that Christian witness is not simply a witness to the resurrection of Jesus Christ, but that it is itself dependent on the risen Lord.

JAMES   That even a person like me talks about Christian

witness is due to the fact that I too believe in what you have described as the nearness of miracle. I know that Jesus makes Himself known, and that I can play my part depending on Him never to let me down.

JOAN   The way you say it, Jim, I think makes the point. We have been talking about the nature of Christian witness and our responsibility for it, but actually the significance of our conversation lies in that we had the conversation at all. Jesus made us talk about this subject. It arose because in a deeper sense than we know, we already belong to Him; and not only we, but everybody else.

The Event

The thrust of the conversation in the last chapter was to raise the question: How does it happen that we are concerned with this matter of Christian witness at all? Why must we reflect upon it? Why do we think of it as part of our responsibility? And the suggestion made in the conversation was that it is because something has happened to us which is, at the same time, part of a wider happening—an event which includes all men in its scope and has consequences for all men. The intention of this chapter is to speak of this happening; to speak not of the gospel-event as such—the story of God become man in Jesus Christ and of Jesus Christ as the man for men; but to speak rather of how we become involved as His witnesses and what that involvement means.

In order to avoid the temptation of a discursive discussion, let us concentrate on a specific biblical text. There occurs in the book of Psalms, four times over, a phrase which is translated "God is my portion." It is a phrase which bears testimony to something that has happened. God and man have become related. The possessive "my" shows how intimate that relationship is. The word "portion" has behind it experiences with God which have spelled out for the men who had them both privilege and duty, both infinite gain and inescapable responsibility. What is the nature of the event which has produced this situation? For only out of such a situation does the concern for witness become a compelling one.

THE PORTION I HAVE CHOSEN

The first occurrence in the book of Psalms of the phrase we shall be meditating on is in Psalm 16. The psalmist here is living among people who worship other gods and whose pressure on him to worship as they worship is a constant one. But says the psalmist, "O God, Thou art my Lord." He has made his choice and by that choice he feels himself bound. "The Lord," he says, "is my chosen portion from the plate, the share of my inheritance." [1] The picture here is of the common plate in which food was served on the table: and those sitting round chose from that plate the portions of meat which they preferred. As the psalmist would put it, other men may choose other things from the common plate of life—position or wealth, comfort or happiness, power or influence—but I have chosen God.

There is a second picture in the way in which the psalmist speaks. Just as when common land is divided by lot, the lot for someone may fall in a "pleasant place"; so God has been alloted to him as the share of his inheritance. Here is testimony to the double nature of the event which constitutes the gospel. It is offered to us but does not become ours unless we choose it. And yet it becomes ours by our having been chosen to possess it. Moffatt translates verse 5 of

[1] This is the meaning of the text as given by the Tamil translation.

Psalm 16 as follows: "Thou art what I get from life. Thou thyself art my share."

An incident in the life of our Lord illustrates what we are talking about. A rich man came to Jesus and said to Him, "Good Master, what must I do to enter into my inheritance —to inherit eternal life?" The answer of Jesus was, "Sell all that you have, give it to the poor and come and follow me." (Mark 10:25). This rich young man not only had great material possessions but he had also great religious achievements. He had kept the law from his youth upwards. By the way Jesus set His demand—"Follow me"—the young man was faced with the choice of possessing Jesus alone. He was not even allowed to give his wealth to Jesus. He had to give it to the poor. Neither was he allowed to make his religious achievements a stepping stone to further obedience. This he could have done if Jesus had given him a law, some further duty to fulfil. But Jesus demanded faith, the decision to make Jesus his companion, his only companion.

The event which we are seeking to understand is this event—the event by which our decision for Christ and His decision about us is stripped of all subsidiary motives. As the psalmist puts it, we come to the point when we say, "Thou art my Lord, my welfare rests on thee alone." (Moffatt). Knox translates, "All the good I possess is nothing compared with the Lord whom I own as my God."

Psalm 16 ends with the words, "Thou dost show me the path of life; in thy presence there is fulness of joy, in thy right hand are pleasures for evermore." Whatever it be that God has in His right hand for us, that is good. The determining fact here is that God who brings the gift is Himself the source of all our joy. Because we have learnt to be happy with Him alone, we find that we can be happy whatever He brings. This note of joy is the true test of whether the event we are talking about has happened to us. It is not that after this, life will not have its sorrows, its trials and its tears; but that these will produce neither despair nor bitterness because they will be sustained by a joy whose source is not in ourselves.

It is futile to undertake the task of Christian witness or to talk about the responsibility of Christian witness, where this joy from an event that has happened to us—the event of having been claimed for the gospel and of having claimed the gospel—does not exist.

THE PORTION THAT REMAINS

The second occurrence of the phrase "God is my portion" is in Psalm 73.

> "When my soul was embittered,
> When I was pricked in heart,
> I was stupid and ignorant,
> I was like a beast toward thee.
>
> My flesh and my heart may fail,
> But God is the strength of my heart
>   and my portion for ever."

The situation in this Psalm is quite different from that in Psalm 16. Here the psalmist is faced with no choices. Grief and disaster have overtaken him. In spite of his faithfulness to God, he has been overwhelmed by trouble. "All in vain," he says, "have I kept my heart clean and washed my hands in innocence. For all the day long I have been stricken, and chastened every morning." Also, he finds himself living among people who have never bothered about God and yet who have prospered. His envy of their condition makes his own condition worse. "I was envious of the arrogant," he confesses, "for they have no pangs; their bodies are sound and sleek."

It is not necessary that this precise experience has to be ours, before this Psalm can have meaning for us. In so many ways life can suddenly become empty of meaning and troubles may be such as to embitter the soul. At such times, the whole edifice of life crumbles. Everything is shaken and the very foundations of life give way.

As I write this, my mind goes to a lady who some time ago came to me for prayer. She had been a Hindu, and in a Christian college had found Jesus as Saviour. Against the wishes of her parents and relations she had accepted baptism. Later, she met and married a Christian young man who belonged to another community than her own. The result was that she was not welcomed into the home of her husband and by his people. Within six months of marriage her husband fell ill and his illness was diagnosed as cancer. She had a child now a year old. When she told me her story, what was there for me to say or do? She said to me, "Pastor, I have even lost my faith. I don't think I believe in Jesus Christ anymore." I prayed with her. Then, just before she left, she said to me, "I am arranging for the baptism of my child next week." Why was she doing it? Within a few months, her husband would be dead. Would it not have been the natural thing for her to go back to her own parents and to her Hindu home. But she could not do it. She was unable to think of doing it because there was one thing in her life which remained unshaken. It was Jesus himself. She had lost her faith in Him, but she had not lost Him. He remained. He always remains. In the words of the psalmist, "He is my portion for ever."

The psalmist is frank to confess that his thoughts are all wrong and that his emotions are all wrong. As far as he is concerned, he has become like one of the animals without any sense of God. "Nevertheless," he says, "I am continually with thee. Thou dost hold my right hand." In the book of Lamentations (3:19), one of the singers breaks away from his remembrance of the "wormwood and the gall" to a celebration of the steadfastness of the Lord.

> "The steadfast love of the Lord never ceases,
> His mercies never come to an end.
> The Lord is my portion, says my soul,
> Therefore I will hope in Him."

The event by which the Christian life is determined is an event through which Jesus Christ becomes part of our life. And once this has happened, He remains in our life that part which nothing can remove. He simply does not go away leaving us alone.

Paul, in his letter to the Corinthians, compares the witness of the Christian life to a sweet smell. (2 Cor. 2:15) This sweet smell comes from the presence of Jesus in our lives. It is a presence we do not control. And the smell is something which we can neither hide nor put on. As far as we are concerned, it is involuntary. Where this involuntary witness is absent our voluntary witness carries little conviction.

THE PORTION COMMITTED TO ME

In the third occurrence of the phrase, "God is my portion," in Psalm 119:57, the event referred to has a different dimension.

> "The Lord is my portion;
> I promise to keep thy words.
> I hasten and do not delay
> To keep thy commandments
> Though the cords of the wicked ensnare me
> I do not forget thy law."

Here is recognition that God is my portion in the simple sense that He has entrusted Himself to me. I have become a steward of the mysteries of God. (1 Cor. 4:1). It is now my responsibility to be true to my trust, to keep His words, to obey His law, to safeguard His honor, to keep Him safe for others.

This is an aspect of Christian witness which is easy to understand but which is very difficult to perform. How often has it been true that others have found it difficult to believe in Jesus Christ because of us. We bring disgrace on His name, we prove disloyal to His work, we betray the Church's fellowship, we do not reflect His glory. To the psalmist, the sign that God had become his portion was that God had given him the statutes. For us the sign is that God has entrusted His work of mercy and forgiveness into our hands. "He has given us the ministry of reconciliation." (2 Cor. 5:18)

The more one looks at the inner meaning of Christian

witness, the more one is convinced that at the heart of it, lies the simple duty of being kind. "Above all else, be kind," says Paul to the Colossians (Col. 3:14). "Put affection into your love," he writes to the Romans. (Rom. 12:10 Moffatt.) But why do we find it so difficult to be kind? Is it not because kindness can be the fruit only of a life that is happy? And true happiness is impossible in this life unless it is happiness in God. An unhappy person is quite willing to make others unhappy. In that willingness lies the seed of unkindness. Love is a duty. We are taught to love our enemies. But affection can never be commanded. To have affection is to find someone else lovable. It is to learn to love others for their own sake. Of course, it is difficult to have affection for certain people. But basic to the task of Christian witness is the fact that Christ loves these people, and His love for them has been entrusted to us. We must learn to pray for such people constantly, because when we pray for people we shall learn to love them also. It is difficult not to love somebody for whom we pray.

In other words, the event that we are speaking about is an event which not only concerns Jesus Christ and us, but concerns others as well. Because of Jesus Christ, they become our neighbours—people whose care is our concern. The emphasis I want to make is not that we are under obligation to love others; but that, willy-nilly, others have become part of our lives because of Jesus Christ. That is the nature of the event that we are talking about. And, because they are part of our lives, they are our trust. God is our portion because He has entrusted himself to us in them. It is no more a question of keeping His statutes. It is now a matter of feeding Him when He is hungry, of clothing Him when He is naked, of visiting Him when He is in prison, of welcoming Him when He is a stranger. (Matt. 25:35f)

Here arises the necessity to see others in Jesus Christ and to see Jesus Christ in others. So often, when we talk of Christian witness, we are too conscious of the fact that we represent Jesus Christ and His gospel. We do. But those to whom we go also represent Jesus Christ and His demands.

THE PORTION WHICH BY ITSELF IS SUFFICIENT

In Psalm 142, where we find, for the fourth time, the use of the phrase, "God is my portion," the situation out of which the psalmist speaks is again a different one from the three previous occurrences. The singer of this psalm is in great trouble. He is surrounded by enemies who seek to ensnare him. "No refuge remains to me, no man cares for me" is his cry. He was not only all alone, but everything he had has been taken away from him. He is like a man in prison. Nothing belongs to him anymore. In this situation, he turns to the Lord. "To thee Lord, I cry," he says, "claiming thee for my only refuge, all that is left me in this world of living men." (Knox). The world is bristling with men, they are very much alive and active. However, even in such a world, there is safety and shelter for him who holds on to God. God alone is left, but God is enough.

The experiences by which men come to recognize the sufficiency of God are many and varied; but they must come to such a recognition, if their testimony to Him is to sound genuine. In the ministry of Jesus, there are many instances where Jesus sought to teach people to desire God alone. Two negative examples will make the point. There is the instance where a man came to Jesus and said to Him,

"Teacher, bid my brother divide the inheritance with me."
(Lk. 12:13) The request was obviously a legitimate one. A
father had died entrusting his property to his eldest son who
had been asked to give a rightful share to his younger
brother. But the older boy had taken it all. Jesus, however,
refuses to do anything about this. Why? Suppose Jesus
should come to anyone of us and say, "Make me one request, the one thing you really want me to do for you,"
—what would you ask Him? Here was this young man able
to make a request of Jesus Christ and what he asks from
Him is land. There is nothing wrong in the request, but it
shows how little the man understood who Jesus was or
cared about what Jesus alone could do. The answer of Jesus
to this man was a double one. He said to him, "Who do you
think I am?" and warned him not to allow possessions to
possess him. A true test of whether we have met Jesus is
what we asked of Him when we met Him.

When Jesus went to Nazareth, says Mark, "He could do
no mighty work there, except that He laid His hands upon a
few sick people and healed them. And he marvelled because
of their unbelief." (Mk. 6:6). Reporting the same incident,
Matthew says, "He did not do many mighty works, because
of their unbelief." (Matt. 13:58). Here was a situation in
which unbelief made it impossible for Jesus to give to His
people what He really wanted to give them. All they wanted
was to be healed of their sicknesses. The response of Jesus
was to refuse to give them even the healings they asked for.
Being who He was, He could not allow them to exploit
Him.

In one way or another, we must come to that encounter
with Him by which we are established in our true relation to

Him: by which we come to recognize in Him, the one whom our soul desires above all else, and the one with whom we shall be content, even if we have Him alone. Fredrick W. H. Myers opens his poem, "St. Paul" with the following three verses:

"Christ I am Christ's and let the name suffice you,
Ay, for me too He greatly hath sufficed;
Lo with no winning words I would entice you,
Paul has no honour and no friend but Christ.

Yes, without cheer of sister or of daughter,
Yes, without stay of father or of son,
Lone on the land and homeless on the water
Pass I in patience till the work be done.

Yet not in solitude if Christ anear me
Waketh Him workers for the great employ,
Oh not in solitude, if souls that hear me
Catch from my joyaunce the surprise of joy."

Christ fills the whole horizon: and the human soul is completely caught up in the divine adventure.

The Choice

In speaking about the event by which Christian life and discipleship are constituted and witness concerning it to others is borne, we have stressed the double nature of that event. It is both what God does and what we do. It is contrived for us by the experiences and circumstances of life, it is also brought upon us by the love and mercy of God. He finds us and we find Him.

In this third chapter, we shall look closely at the nature of the human response which is part of the event that we have been speaking about. It is important to do this for not only is our response previous to the life of witness, but it is itself part of that witness. What men must be able to see is the way in which our own lives are lived in Jesus Christ. We often make the mistake of thinking that others will be able to read our lives from a distance. Certainly, there are saints who are so obviously saints that even from a distance they can be recognized as men who walk with God. But most of

us are not that kind of person. No one will see God's grace
at work in us, unless he or she is able to, is allowed to, get
close enough to us to see. We must live with people, the
people among whom we desire to witness. We must know
them and they must know us within one common life and
then, by God's mercy, some of them will see in us, the
working of God's grace. They will see how by that grace we
do what is good, we avoid what is bad, we overcome temptation, we repent when we sin, we struggle until that sin has
no more power over us. They will see how we are upheld by
God even when we have lost our hold on Him, and that we
are remembered by Him even when we have forgotten Him.

The Christian life is rooted in a choice and is constantly
carried forward by choices. Let us seek to understand the
nature of this choice and its consequent choices, remembering that what we are seeking to understand is how this experience is itself a witness to the ways of God with men.

In Paul's second letter to the Thessalonians, there is a
discussion about the coming of our Lord Jesus Christ in
glory (2 Thes. 2:1-12.) Speaking about it, Paul insists that
before the day of the Lord comes "the man of lawlessness
must be revealed." However difficult it may be to say exactly what Paul had in mind, the implication of what he
says is clear. Every man has a decisive choice to make, and
there will be no foreclosure of history which will render it
unnecessary for some to make this choice. Men must
choose, they will be made to choose, between the person
and activity of Jesus Christ and the person and activity of
the lawless one. Whom will they trust, in whom will they
believe, by whom are they prepared to live?

This choice, says Paul, will be a real one, because the

lawless one too has his credentials. "He will come with all power and with pretended signs and wonders." Were life in Jesus Christ man's only option, then there would be no problem. The problem is that there are workable alternatives to faith in Jesus Christ, at least as far as this life is concerned. However, they who "love the truth," says Paul, will not be deceived by any of these alternatives. They are so committed already that no one else and nothing else is able to shake that commitment. Falling in love is a very decisive experience. It means a radical shift of focus and perspective in one's life. But what is more important is, it means the willingness of the lover to give himself or herself away to the beloved. What love accomplishes, when we fall in love, is that we no more belong to ourselves.

Central to the Christian life is an experience to which the term "Conversion" has been given. Behind this word "Conversion" lie two ideas: the one is associated with the word "repentance" and the other with the word "return." To repent is to go through a process of transformation. By it a past is rejected and the transformed person begins to live in terms of a new point of orientation. To return is to realize that the new which one has accepted is that to which one naturally belongs. God's love and mercy have all the time been the determining circumstance of one's life: to this love and mercy, man returns in willing acknowledgment and glad surrender.

The word "love" is the most appropriate to encompass both ideas. "The truth must be loved." Indeed, it must be loved because the truth is a person—Jesus Christ. To love Jesus Christ is to turn away from the lawless one, whoever he is and under whatever guise he comes. Every rival to

Jesus Christ for our love must be rejected. Also, to love Him is to return to Him; for He is the eternal Lover. He loved us from the beginning with an unwearied love.

The common New Testament word which is used to signify this act of choice, this act of repentance and return, this act of love, is the word "believe." Wherever and whenever the gospel is proclaimed, the command addressed to the hearer is "believe." But, precisely because the command arises from the gospel, its obedience too is dependent on the gospel. God's love towards us is what makes the act of believing possible. We believe because of what God has already done.

There are many ways of seeking to understand what the New Testament means by "believing." For myself, I have always found illumination in the actual ways in which in the Greek language, the New Testament writers use the verb "believe" and the many pictures which, by this usage, they suggest. The verb "believe" in the Greek is always followed by a preposition of location or motion, the preposition used putting the noun which it governs either in the accusative case or the dative case. This difference of case in the Greek, whereas in English the objective case is the only one, makes it easier to bring out shades of meaning. By this not only is the object of belief pointed out but what belief implies is also explained.

JESUS IS GOD'S PLACE OF APPOINTMENT
TO BELIEVE IS TO TAKE ONE'S PLACE IN HIM

In Mark's gospel the opening proclamation of our Lord is given in these terms: "The Kingdom of God has drawn near. It has come so near that to stretch out one's hand is to be able to touch it. Therefore, men must turn around and believe in the good news." (Mk. 1:15) The preposition used with the verb "believe" in this instance, is the preposition "en" followed by the dative. The Kingdom of God is a reality within which one must live. To repent is so to turn around that one is able to see what God has done; and to believe is to take one's place within it. The Kingdom must be so accepted that it becomes one's dwelling place. The idea emphasized is one of location.

Behind the verb "believe" and the noun "faith," as they are used by the New Testament writers, lies the conviction that it was the Kingdom of God which verily had come to them and to the world in Jesus Christ. It had come crashing into their lives and into the life of the world. God's reign had become visible and tangible in the Christ-event. "That which we have seen and heard," says John, "we proclaim also to you." And the proclamation is to this end—"that you may have fellowship with us, whose fellowship is with the Father and with His Son, Jesus Christ." (1 John 1:3)

"To believe in" is so to learn to live within the Kingdom and to live by it that one's life is determined by one's loyalties to it, is enriched by its blessings and is empowered by its resources. Or, to use another picture, "to believe in" is to abide in Jesus Christ who is the vine and of whom we are the branches. (John 15:5) How often we say to one another and to ourselves, "I could not help it. After all, I am only human. It was only natural that I said it or felt it or did it." "The gospel," says Paul, "is the power of God and the wisdom of God to them that are being saved." (1 Cor. 1:18)

To be in the Kingdom is to be in this process of salvation. It is to know of its power and to live by its wisdom.

In Paul's letter to the Ephesians, we have another example of the use of the preposition "en," where the object of faith is described as the Lord Jesus. The realm where Christ is Lord is where the Christian must learn to dwell and, as Paul puts it, with this faith must go "love toward all the saints." (Eph. 1:15) The relation established by faith is never with Jesus alone, it is also with all those who belong to Him. To be in the Kingdom is to know oneself as part of a company of believers, as a member of the household of faith.

JESUS IS THE SPRING OF A NEW SOCIETY
TO BELIEVE IS TO ENTER IT AND BELONG TO IT

The act of entrance into this society is the second picture which is suggested by the word "believe." Whenever the preposition "eis" followed by the accusative is used with the verb "believe," it is a movement which is shown as taking place. In John's gospel, at the close of the story of the miracle at the wedding feast at Cana, the evangelist says, "This, the first of His signs, Jesus did at Cana in Galilee, and manifested His glory; and His disciples believed into Him." (John. 2:11) The sign pointed the way to a new possibility, and the disciples followed it. They left the society to which they always belonged and entered into the society of Jesus. From now on, they belonged to one another and to Him. They became the nucleus of the new ecclessia.

In the incident concerning the conversion of Cornelius, the speech of Peter concludes with these words. "To Him all the prophets bear witness, that everyone who believes into Him receives forgiveness of sins through His name." (Acts 10:43) Here again, what happens is that Cornelius and his friends enter into a new relationship with God and with men made possible by the Holy Spirit. God has provided for man a new starting point in Jesus Christ. By it, men are challenged to a new adventure. When Paul asked the disciples at Ephesus whether they had received the Holy Spirit, and they answered "no," his question to them was, "Into what then were you baptized?" (Acts 19:3) They answered that the baptism which they had received was the baptism of John: whereupon Paul said to them, "But did not John point to Jesus Christ?" The baptism of repentance simply set one's feet on a journey. It was Jesus Christ who was that journey's destination. To turn around was not enough, one had to enter.

We can see here the emphasis placed by the New Testament proclamation not only on the affirmation that, in Jesus, the Kingdom of God had come; but also on the experience that in Him the reign of God remained continuously explosive. Indeed, it was by this continuous explosion that the movement of faith was both initiated and maintained.

JESUS IS LIFE'S LONE FOUNDATION
TO BELIEVE IS TO BUILD ON HIM

As we have seen, the preposition "en" followed by the dative suggests the picture of where the believer must dwell and that by which he must learn to live; while the preposition "eis" followed by the accusative suggests the picture of the society into which the believer must enter and the destination towards which he is set. The third picture which we have is given to us by the use of the preposition "epi" also followed by the accusative. In the story of Calvary, we read that the spectators around the cross said to one another, "If He will come down from the cross, we shall believe upon Him." (Matt. 27:42) In the story of Dorcas, we are told that when she was brought to life by Peter, its sequel was that many believed upon Him. (Acts 9:42) In both these instances, the picture suggested is of Jesus as the foundation of men's lives. In Him is power adequate for every circumstance. He is Master of every situation, including death: so that to build our lives upon Him is to build securely, to make Him our standing ground is to stand where one does not slip. To believe is not only to be located within but to be located upon.

In the story of the Phillipian jailer, as we find it in the Acts of the Apostles, we have an incident in which a man is suddenly faced with a situation in which he may not only lose his job but also his life. He asks Paul the question, "What must I do to be safe?" Paul's answer is, "Build your faith upon Jesus Christ and then you will be safe: safe even if you lose your job, safe even if you lose your life; and not only safe yourself but also your wife and your children." (Acts 16:30, 31). To build upon Jesus is to build against every eventuality.

There is also a further consequence of this fact that it is on Jesus that we must build, for so to do means that the pattern of the house of our lives is already set. The foundation determines the shape of the building. What is this shape? The answer of the gospel story is that the pattern reads as follows: a borrowed manger, the public street, an upper room, a lonely garden, the hill outside the city, an open tomb. To build our lives upon Jesus Christ is to accept these as determining also the pattern of our own lives.

Is there an alternative? Jesus said that there was. He said that one could build on sand or on rock. To build on sand was easier. Besides, for many years the river-bed had remained dry, so that the risk of a flood was a risk that could be taken. On the other hand, to build on rock was harder. It would cost more. But faith must choose: choose whether to build on rock or on sand, whether to listen to Jesus and obey or, having listened to Him, to disobey nevertheless. (Matt. 7:24-27)

In this insistence, that to have faith was to come to terms with an unchangeable fact, the New Testament bears witness to the secular quality of the Christ-event. Were the Christ-event only a religious event, its truth would be dependent on men's acknowledgment and acceptance of it. But being an event within the very texture of human history and embracing in its consequences the whole of creation, it defines the situation within which men must live and with which men must reckon. By its very secularity, it exerts pressure on the human will and the human mind.

JESUS IS HOME
TO BELIEVE IS TO COME TO REST WITHIN

But, when the verb "believe" is followed by the preposition "epi," not only the accusative but also the dative is used. The picture which the dative suggests is of the soul come to rest. In his first letter to Timothy, Paul refers to his life before he knew Jesus. He speaks of the utter restlessness of it and of the rebellion by which it was characterised. "But," he says, "God's patience found me. The grace of our Lord overflowed for me with the faith and love that are in Christ Jesus." Paul had found his rest and, "this," he says to his readers, "can be your experience also." (1 Tim. 1:12-16)

Peter in his letter quoted from the Old Testament the saying about the corner stone. Here again the verb "believe" is followed by "epi" with the dative. "Behold, I am laying in Zion a stone, a corner stone chosen and precious, and he who believes in him will not be put to shame." (1 Peter 2:6) All anxieties are over, life has found its harmony, the corner stone has knit the building together, the soul is at rest. Paul, quoting this same passage from the Old Testament, draws out the contrast between believing in the law and believing in Jesus Christ. "To believe in the law," he says, "is to be let down. For the law cannot save or make safe. Whereas to believe in Jesus Christ is, indeed, not to be put to shame." (Rom. 9:33)

The picture here is of that inner experience which belongs to the life of faith. When the Kingdom came in Jesus Christ, not only did it come crashing into men's lives and demanding from them a decisive decision, but it also showed with complete clarity how wonderful and all sufficient and unconditional was the love of God. It was by this love that those who so responded found their rest. It is not so much that one places faith on Christ, as that one is placed on Christ. There is indication here of the passivity of the Christian experience. To exercise faith is also to know that that faith is given. Just as a mother picks up her baby, so God picks us up and places us on himself and there, in our mother's arms, we come to rest.

JESUS OFFERS THE MOST INCLUSIVE FELLOWSHIP
TO BELIEVE IS TO ACCEPT THIS OFFER

There is still another preposition with which the verb "believe" is used. It is the preposition "pros" with the accusative. The most significant illustration of the force of this preposition is found in the opening declaration of John's gospel. "In the beginning was the Word, and the Word was toward God." (John 1:1) To be toward was to be face to face.

The emphasis here is on the relationship of fellowship, of being open towards one another. To believe is to turn towards and to remain face to face. Paul, in his first letter to the Thessalonians, says to them, "You became imitators of us and of the Lord": and then he goes on, "your faith toward God has gone forth everywhere." (1 Thess. 1:6-8) What had gone forth and become a public witness was the evidence that here were men living in a face to face relationship with God. His reflection was seen in them, and their imitation of Paul was part of this reflection. In his letter to Philemon, Paul expresses this same idea. He speaks of Philemon as "having faith toward the Lord Jesus and into all the saints." (Phil. 5) The implication of what Paul is saying, and the way he is saying it, is clear. When one's faith is toward the Lord Jesus it must issue in a movement into the fellowship of those who belong to Him.

So we come to the close of this study, recognising that the pictures we have looked at shade into one another, until we arrive finally at the picture which shows the believer standing face to face with his Lord. The vision of the Master is the true end of faith.

John finds this notion of faith, of believing, so radical that he compares it to a new birth, a birth from above. For faith is never man's possibility. Paul compares it to a death and resurrection. Birth and death are both violent symbols, but the act of faith does contain within it an act of violence. "The kingdom of God suffers violence," said Jesus, "and the violent take it by force." (Matt. 11:12)

The Family

When the disciples asked Jesus to teach them to pray, He taught them an actual prayer. It set them within the only context within which any kind of responsibility to God and fellowman can be either understood or discharged. The responsibility for Christian witness is no exception. Those to whom we would witness are already members with us in one family. So that it is within the total nexus of relationships within that family that Christian witness can be truly borne. In Christian witnessing, we think so easily and naturally of "we" and "they." We forget so easily that the relationship of encounter and dialogue has to be held within a common life, that "we" and "they" already belong together in such a life, and that this common life is not only our life in this world but also our life in God. In prayer and participation in this common life is the main substance of Christian witness.

We have already made the point that we must live close enough to people, so that they can see us as we really are.

Indeed, the power of Christian witness does not lie in people seeing how good we are, but rather in people being able to see how God's grace and judgment operate in our lives. They must see how He deals with us and we deal with Him, and how we find room in our affection and concern for those He brings to us, as the good Samaritan brought the wounded wayfarer to the innkeeper. Christian witness is the testimony of the whole story of our lives with all their lights and shadows, warts and all.

There is no better description of the nature of our common life, our life within the Christian family as well as the human family, than is contained in the family prayer which the Lord taught His disciples. Let us look at this prayer and see what it says. (Matt. 6:9-13)

A COMMON FATHER—A COMMON LIFE

The prayer begins with the words "Our Father." The first thing to remember here is that it is Jesus who is telling us to call God Father. The father-child relationship between God and man is not a relationship which can be taken for granted. The prodigal son, when he came back home, came to his father with the words, "I have sinned." (Lk. 15:21) Sin must be dealt with before the child's call to the father can be a glad one. So that when Jesus tells us to call God Father it is because in Him the relationship of man to God is restored. "To as many as received Him to them He gave authority to call themselves the children of God." (John 1:12) So that, when we say that this is the prayer which our Lord taught us, we also mean that we can pray it because it was He who taught it to us.

The Father who is addressed is called "Our Father." The 'our' is primarily the Christian family, but it is also the human family. Whether others know God as Father or not, we know that they are His children and that we cannot go to Him without our brethren, our fellowmen. In this form of address is defined the origin and scope of our common life.

LIFE'S BOUNDARIES—HIS NAME, HIS REIGN, HIS WILL

The three statements which follow define the boundaries of our human living and striving: "Thy Name be Hallowed, Thy Kingdom come, Thy Will be done." Couched though these are in the form of petitions, they affirm three truths which are already true. God's name is Holy. God's Kingdom has come. God's will is being done. These are already real "in heaven." The petitions are concerned with making these actual on earth. It is not that heavenly reality is not part of earthly reality, but that it is not yet manifestly so.

God's Name is what He has revealed of Himself to us. This revelation we may never treat lightly. It sets out for us one of the boundaries of our life which we may not cross. Some know more of that Name than others, while some do not know the Name at all. These address their longings and unuttered prayers to Him whom they can only call "the Unknown God." Yet, by this very act of calling Him "the Unknown God," they keep on this side of the boundary. They obey the injunction that God's Name should remain hallowed.

Another boundary which limits human life and freedom is the reign of God. Men have a consciousness of freedom. They will and they perform. But everytime we pray "Thy

Kingdom come," we acknowledge that man's freedom has its limitations. God maintains His rule. He rules and over-rules. It is certainly true that in the world, the rule of God is constantly being contested by evil in many forms. But some day, this contest will be over. Indeed, the issue of this contest is never in doubt. So that when we pray, "Thy Kingdom come," we are praying for the triumph of God's rule on earth now in every contest, and the final triumph of that rule when God's Kingdom would have come in glory.

But He who is God and Lord has chosen man to work with Him and for Him, so that human life has been invested with a divine significance. Our work has within it the possibility of becoming a testimony to Him. He has employed us in His service. He has consented to reveal to us His plans. He is prepared to be patient with us as we strive to do His will. Jesus said, when you pray, ask that those on earth should do God's will as faithfully as those in heaven. The will of God is also a boundary of man's life. It is the boundary which moment by moment we must seek to keep, knowing that transgression is sin.

The phrase "On earth as it is in heaven," is a phrase which qualifies all three petitions. It is what makes these petitions not pious hopes, but a conscious recognition of the basic structure of human life. The truth about our world is that in it, God has made Himself known, maintains His rule and invites men to do His will. This action of God is independent of our praying. We pray as we do because that is the way to acknowledge what life is really like. Nor must we forget that these three petitions are petitions in the plural. The hallowing of His name, the waiting for His Kingdom, the doing of His will are never an individual occupation. In all three, all men are involved. Some know what they are doing, some do not. But all are involved together in a common life, whose boundaries for all of them are defined by these three petitions.

LIFE'S NEEDS—FOOD, FORGIVENESS, WORK

The Lord's prayer moves from an acknowledgment of life's boundaries to requests concerning life's basic needs. The first need for life is food: "Give us this day our daily bread." It is right that the material needs of life should be God's concern. It is right that we should know that they are His concern and should, therefore, ask Him to provide them. But here again, it is important to remember that the prayer is in the plural. I know that God provides bread for me only as He provides bread for others. When I pray for daily bread, I am praying for the farmer who sows the grain, I am praying for the engineer who builds the tanks from which water flows to irrigate the fields, I pray for the banks which give the loans to the farmers and to the co-operatives who buy the grain and market it. Indeed, I am praying for the whole world economy.

We are told that the word translated 'daily' is a technical word used to describe a soldier's ration. If this is so, it is easy to see how closely connected the prayer for bread is to the doing of God's will. Our right to pray for bread rests on our willingness to be soldiers in His service. It may be true that many who are not soldiers in God's service do nevertheless get bread. But that has nothing to do with the actual implications of the prayer.

It is perhaps necessary to say one thing more about this

prayer for bread. And that is to remind ourselves of the way in which how, over and over again, God answers this prayer. There was a boy who believed in prayer but he was poor and hungry and ill-clothed. His friends said to him one day, "What is the use of prayer, seeing that you go hungry most of the time?" His answer was, "God has told somebody to give me bread and that somebody always forgets." Perhaps, in the case of most of us, we don't forget so completely. There is a verse which says:

"I asked God for a loaf of bread, He gave me two,
One for my neighbour and one for myself,
    and I kept both."

Perhaps, it would be truer to say that God gave me three, two for my neighbours and one for myself and I kept two. We may not pray for bread without being willing to fulfil our responsibility in the common life.

Bread is one of life's basic needs. The second which the Lord's Prayer points up is forgiveness. "Forgive us our trespasses as we forgive those who trespass against us." Life would become insupportable, if there were no way of getting rid of our sins. When one has done something wrong, what a relief it is to be able to go to father or mother, teacher or principal, employer or colleague, and confess to them what one has done. Then when punishment has been meted out or warning given, when the fellowship that wrongdoing has broken has been restored, what a relief it is.

But firmly linked to the prayer for forgiveness is the statement "as we forgive others." We misunderstand this connection between God's forgiveness and our forgivingness when we think of it as a contract or bargain. God does not say, "I shall forgive you only if you forgive others": rather, the point is that God has already forgiven us and them, so that we enter into the experience of God's forgiveness of us only as we enter also into participation in God's forgiveness of others.

Forgiveness is past tense. God has paid the price of it. It has been wrought for us and for all men on Calvary's hill, where Jesus loved to the uttermost. But precisely as forgiveness is past tense, it is also indivisible. I cannot have my own little bit of forgiveness apart from the total forgiving activity of God. Those who have sinned against me, in that they sinned, have really sinned against God. But God has forgiven them. So that when I refuse to forgive them, I can only do so by refusing to participate in God's forgiveness of them. The consequence of such a refusal is that I have to forego the experience of my forgiveness too. Indeed, it is at this point that the specific meaning of forgiveness as a Christian experience becomes clear. To be forgiven by God in Christ is not simply to be rid of one's guilt, it is to enter into the forgiving activity of God.

We have already seen how important it is to recognize that prayer for bread has meaning only in the plural. It is prayer within the common life. The prayer for forgiveness is not less so.

The third need which is basic to human living is work. We cannot live without bread, we cannot live without forgiveness, also we cannot live without something to do. We speak of the right of the citizen to find employment. When there is unemployment in a country, that is a blot on that country's government. The Lord's Prayer acknowledges this fact of employment; of God calling us and using us, giving each his own employment and to each his work.

In the gospel story, we are told that immediately after His baptism, He was led by the Holy Spirit into the wilderness to be tempted by the devil. (Matt. 4:1) It is by the devil that He was tempted. It was by the Holy Spirit that He was led to the place of temptation. The place of our appointment is also the place of our temptation. There are always the temptations that are incident on the work which God has given us to do. It is this that is recognised in the prayer, "Lead us not into temptation."

The point of the prayer is that we should never be so self-confident that we can tell God that we are ready or adequate for our encounter with Evil. Sometimes in school, a teacher may say to his pupils, "Today we are going to have a test in arithmetic or history. It is going to be a surprise test." The pupils have the right to say, "Not today, teacher, we are not ready." The prayer, "Lead us not into temptation," acknowledges our unreadiness, our weakness, our lack of confidence. That is right. No one must pride himself that he stands, lest he fall. However, we cannot always be spared our times of testing. Surprise tests are part of God's provision in the school of life. So that we not only pray "Lead us not into temptation," but we also pray "Deliver us from evil," or "deliver us from the evil one." When we do come to our moments of contest with evil, we can stand only in His strength, find shelter only in His mercy and deliverance only in Him.

Here again we need to remember that in these contests with evil in the course of our work, we shall never be alone because we never work alone. There are our companions on the way, our colleagues and our co-workers. When we pray for ourselves, we pray for them also. They belong with us in this prayer of the servant to his Master.

LIFE'S CERTAINTIES—HIS KINGDOM, POWER AND GLORY

To this prayer which our Lord taught us, the Church has added a doxology: "For Thine is the Kingdom the Power and the Glory, for ever and ever." The thrust of this doxology is to point to the certainties on which the prayer is based. In the prayer itself the petition is made, "Thy Kingdom come." In the doxology, the affirmation is made that the Kingdom is already His. In the prayer, the petition is made, "Thy will be done." In the doxology, the affirmation is made that the power is His. In the prayer, petition is made for the gifts God's love will provide. In the doxology, the affirmation is made that the glory is His. There is no doubt about the splendor of His love.

The possibility of the Christian life and the faithfulness of Christian witness do not depend on human effort. In the last analysis, the Christian life is lived exactly in the same way as a person sees. It is the existence of light and color which make sight possible. The eye is made for the light. It sees naturally. Our response to God in faithful Christian living is the natural consequence of what God Himself is. The imperative mood of the Christian ethic is rooted in the indicative mood of the Christian gospel. It is not a question of living a certain kind of life and fulfilling certain kinds of obligations in order to be acceptable to God. It is, on the

other hand, living the kind of life and fulfilling those obligations which are the consequence of having been accepted.

The doxology also points to the certainty of the end. The
Kingdom, the Power, and the Glory are His. They will remain His, until at the end they are seen and acknowledged
as His. "For from Him and through Him and to Him are all
things." (Rom. 11:36) When the writer of the epistle to the
Hebrews speaks of Jesus, not only as the author but also as
the finisher of the race we must run, he is saying something
very important. (Heb. 12:12) The baton that has been put
into our hands is the baton He carried. He began the race.
God sent Him into the world on His mission. Jesus says to
His disciples, "As the Father sent me, so I send you." (John
20:21) So is the baton passed from hand to hand and generation to generation. We run our lap of the race, watched
and encouraged by the witnesses who have run the race
before us. But finally, the person who carries the baton to
the finishing post is Jesus himself.

> "He the prize and He the goal
> and by Him the race begun,
> He the runner of the team who
> will complete the race I run."

Here lies not only the certainty that the race will be com-
pleted but that it will be won. He will bless the work of our
hands, while we work; and then when our work is done He
will establish it. (Ps. 90:17)

The point of this chapter is not just to study the meaning
and scope of the Lord's prayer; it is rather to see, through
such a study, the meaning and scope of our common life;

for Christian witness has to be borne within that common life. Christian witness is a consequence of the way we live it. There is a place in Christian witness for talking about Jesus, there is an equal place for not talking about Him, for just getting on with the job in hand. The miracle is that, even because of us, others are prompted to inquire about Jesus. When this happens then is the time to break our silence.

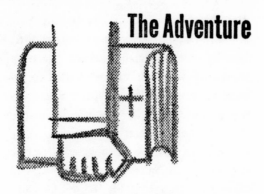

The Adventure

We have looked at the nature of the event out of which the activity of Christian witness arises and by which it is sustained. We have sought to make clear what is involved in the Christian response to the gospel, for on the evidence of that response will depend how credible our Christian witness is. We have also seen that the true context of Christian witness is the common life which we live with our fellow-men. It will now be our attempt to ask and answer a double question: What is the aim of Christian witness? And, what must we expect to happen to us by the very fact that we are witnesses?

THE CONVERSION EXPERIENCE

As an aid to answer the first question, we shall speak pragmatically of the Church's actual ministry of preaching, teaching, and service and what it intends by that ministry. The word in common use for what the Church intends should happen as a consequence of its ministry is the word "Conversion." But it is that very word which needs definition.

If I were describing the aspects of the Christian mission, as one would see it on the Indian scene or on the Ceylon scene, I would distinguish between three main forms of activity. There are, first of all, the preaching and teaching of the Church which are intended to bring a saving knowledge of Jesus Christ to those who hear the message. Secondly, there are the Church's ministries of service which bring to men, in their needs, the succour of God—in relieving pain, in healing sickness, in lifting ignorance, in satisfying hunger, in restoring the lost, and in all those forms of caring which make life bearable and meaningful to the orphan and the widow, the aged and the infirm, the outcast and the refugee. And thirdly, there are those forms of community life within which the Church's proclamation is made, or its service rendered, such as the congregation, the school, the hospital, the orphanage, and so on.

As a result of this threefold impact of the gospel, men and women find themselves brought to the experience of conversion, and find also that this experience has within it a threefold strand. In the first place, there is the experience of conversion to Jesus Christ in which Jesus is acknowledged as personal Lord and Saviour, and where He is confessed as God Incarnate, the only Saviour of all men and the Lord of all life. It will not be incorrect to use the word "evangelism" to denote that aspect of the Church's mission which is intended towards this result.

But, there is also another strand in the conversion experience in which all that happens is that the teaching and example of Christ are accepted as the norm of human living. There are many of whom this is true, who at the same time find themselves unable necessarily to accept the teaching of the Church concerning the person of Jesus Christ. In speaking of this aspect of the conversion experience it will not be incorrect to use the word "Christianization" to denote those activities of the Church which issue in this result.

And then, there is that strand in the conversion experience when men are drawn to the life of the Christian community and decide to become members of it. The normal act through which this is done is the act of baptism. That aspect of the Church's work, by which this change of group allegiance is effected, can rightfully be called "proselytization."

Let us look at some concrete examples of how these three take place. A Hindu student in a Christian College, should he become a Christian, usually goes through the conversion experience in this order: he is first christianized, then evangelized and then proselytized. Most often the conversion experience, when it is the result of the Christian mission as it is prosecuted in a village community, follows a different order. People are first proselytized, then evangelized and then christianized. The conversion experience can happen also in a still different order. A person can first be evangelized, then be proselytized and then be christianized. This is the normal order in which conversion takes place when it is the result of the work of personal evangelism in all its forms.

The point I am trying to make is a simple one: that all these three parts of the conversion experience must become true for all men, and that the order in which they happen does not matter. To be a Christian is to be committed to God in Jesus Christ, it is to belong to the Christian community, and it is to be under compulsion to live a certain kind of life.

THE CONSEQUENCES OF DISCIPLESHIP

Let us now turn to the second question which more directly concerns the adventure on which a Christian embarks when he sets out to be a witness to his Lord, to live the witnessing life as His disciple. Here again, I want to restrict myself to the study of a particular text. It is a text that occurs four times over as spoken by our Lord, and which, it has often seemed to me in its fourfold context, describes accurately the consequences of Christian discipleship. In the gospels, Jesus is reported to have taught His disciples what it would mean to be His servants, and on each occasion to have clinched His argument with the words, "A servant is not greater than his Lord." In the word "servant" is the secret of the witnessing life. For Christian witness is the attempt to live out the servant-role. Our Master is the servant of men. We witness to Him as we seek to be His servants in serving others.

1. *Fidelity under all circumstances:* The first reference is in Matthew's gospel. This is how the passage reads:

> "A disciple is not above his teacher, nor a servant above his master; it is enough for the disciple to be like his teacher, and the servant like his master. If they have called the master of the house Beelzebub, how much more will they malign those of his house-hold?" (Matt. 10:24, 25)

This passage occurs within the context of the sending out of the twelve on their first mission. They went with power to heal the sick, to raise the dead, to cleanse lepers, and to cast out demons. They went with the commission to announce the arrival of the Kingdom. But, says Jesus to them, "Do not be surprised if your ministry in spite of its power and authority, does not convince people that your message is of God and that you are God's messengers. Remember that they called me Beelzebub, so that it is likely that they will put the wrong construction on the things which you shall do also."

One of the constant problems with which we deal and with which we shall continue to deal is how to make the Church's witness successful. This is a question which should never be sidestepped. We must so work and witness that the gospel is commended in power, so that men may be moved to repentance and are led to conversion. But the warning of the Master should also always be remembered, that faithful evangelism will not necessarily win acceptance. It is when this warning is forgotten that methods of successful evangelism are devised, which are simply intended, as it were, to sell the gospel. There is little point in seeking to win men's hearing by adopting new techniques of communication or a new vocabulary, if that which men hear when they listen is a muffled note and not the clear tone of the gospel message.

2. *Concern for people as people:* The second passage in which the text we are studying occurs is in Luke's gospel. It reads as follows:

> "Can a blind man lead a blind man? Will they not both fall into a pit? A disciple is not above his teacher, but everyone when he is fully taught will be like his teacher. Why do you see the speck that is in your brother's eye, but do not notice the log

that is in your own eye? Or, how can you say to your
brother, Brother, let me take out the speck that is
in your eye; when you yourself do not see the log
that is in your own eye? You hypocrite, first take
the log out of your own eye, and then you will see
clearly to take out the speck that is in your
brother's eye." (Luke 6:39-42)

The context within which this passage occurs is that of
our Lord's teaching on forgiveness and mercy. If anyone
was clear sighted, it was our Lord: but how fogiving He was
and how merciful! When He judged it was not to condemn
but to convert. When he criticized, it was because His love
and concern compelled Him.

One of the best-loved theological teachers in India, Dr.
Larsen, used to say, "You must earn the right to criticize."
Where there is no concern for the person who is in the
wrong, criticism is simply indulgence of one's own appetite
for gossip or an expression of one's self-righteousness. Jesus
says to His disciples, "Why should a blind man follow you?
He knows that you are blind too. Why should anyone allow
you to take the speck that is in his eye, when he knows that
you cannot see clearly anyway? Don't you realize that he
can see the log that is in your own eye?"

It is true—is it not?—that so often the note of judgment
in our speaking does not correspond to the example set by
our Master. We stand so far removed from the actual situation which we condemn. It is not that we must not condemn
where concern makes condemnation necessary; but that,
when the word of condemnation has been spoken, we must
find ways of expressing that concern in meaningful involve-

ment, as well as in so applying the word of condemnation to ourselves that we shall seek to remove the log that is in our own eye. To judge must go hand in hand with the willingness to be judged.

3. *A love that does not quit:* The third occasion on which our Lord used this saying that a servant is not greater than his Lord, was in connection with His act in the upper room, when he washed His disciples' feet. On the way to Jerusalem, during that last journey, the disciples sensed that Jesus was moving to the climax of His ministry. The Kingdom of God was going to be established, so that they began quarrelling with one another on the way concerning the place which each wanted to occupy in the Kingdom. When they reached the house where they were to dine together, they refused to perform the common courtesy of pouring water on each other's feet. When Jesus came into the room and noticed what had happened, He washed the feet of them all.

The story of Peter's conversation with his Master, which is part of this incident, is used by John to point out the fact that, among those whose feet were washed, was Judas also. There were eleven whose feet were washed, who needed only that feet washing. "He who has bathed, does not need to wash, except for his feet." But there was a twelfth man, to whom Jesus referred, when He added, "you are clean— but not all of you. He who ate my bread has lifted his heel against me." But even so, the Master washed the feet of Judas.

There is a woodcut by Gross in which Jesus is shown washing one foot of a man who is standing, whose other foot is placed on the neck of Jesus. And, on the face of that man, is a snarl. To do as Jesus did can lead to either the denial of a Peter or the betrayal of a Judas. But precisely in this situation is the teaching apposite, that a servant is not greater than his Master.

Let us listen to the way in which John tells the story:

> "During supper, when the devil had already put it into the heart of Judas Iscariot, Simon's son, to betray him, Jesus knowing that He had come from God and was going to God, began to wash the disciples' feet. When he had washed their feet, he said to them, "I have given you an example that you also should do as I have done to you. Truly, truly, I say to you, a servant is not greater than his master. Nor is he who is sent greater than he who sent him." (John 13:1-16)

4. *The patience to suffer:* The fourth reference of the text which we are studying is also in John's gospel. This is how the passage reads:

> "This I command you, to love one another. If the world hates you, know that it has hated me before it hated you. If you are of the world the world would love its own; but because you are not of the world, but I chose you out of the world, therefore the world hates you. Remember the word that I said to you, 'A servant is not greater than his master.'" (John 15:17-20)

The passage from Matthew's gospel speaks of the possibility of the Christian disciple being misunderstood and maligned. Here in John, the possibility is emphasized of the Christian disciple being hated and persecuted. But what is significant, in the way in which it is put by John, is that this hate and persecution will be the consequence that will accrue to a community that seeks to live in obedience to the command "Love one another."

Nothing is more exasperating than to be loved by someone by whom you do not want to be loved. Our Master told us that if we should love as He commanded us to do, we would produce precisely this kind of exasperation. "They hated me without a cause" is the Scripture which John quotes, when speaking of the hate which Jesus encountered. How pure our love must be and how patient if, even in some measure, this Scripture is to be true of us also!

We said that in this study of the text we have chosen, our attempt will be to look at the nature of the Church's witness and service, and through it to see what it means to say that our objective is the conversion experience. How does it happen that men are converted? What must be the scope and quality of the Church's ministry in the world, if it is to constitute faithful obedience in mission?

The answer that is given to us through the Scripture we have studied is crucial.

> Ours must be a ministry of power, though even such a ministry will be misunderstood and maligned. We are called upon to erect signs of the Kingdom, though many may still read the signs wrong.

Ours must also be a ministry of mercy in which the gospel of forgiveness is both proclaimed and lived out: remembering, however, that we shall not escape the responsibility to criticize, to pronounce judgment; and that therefore every judgment which is pronounced is also binding on ourselves.

Ours too is the ministry of service, of humility and humiliation, whatever the response to such a ministry may be. There will always be that situation in which we are needed and yet not wanted, and therefore a situation in which we must remain because obedience demands it.

And lastly, ours is above all the ministry of patient loving, which alone can make fragrant all the other things which we must do.

In the film on the life of St. Vincent de Paul, the last words of the saint as spoken to a young novice are, "Love them, they will then forgive you your charity." That gets to the heart of the problem. Somehow, men and women everywhere, whom we seek to convert to faith in Christ, whom we seek to win to His allegiance, to whom we minister in His name, are finding it difficult to forgive us—to forgive us not only our weakness but also our strength, to forgive us not only our poverty but also our plenty, to forgive us not only our sins but also our virtues, to forgive us not only our prejudices but also our perceptiveness, to forgive us not only our lack of concern but also our concern. How to win this forgiveness is the heart of the question we are studying.

The Alternative

The concern of Christian witness is that men must choose Jesus Christ. Can we make clear to ourselves and others what it means so to choose?

THE CHOICE

But why put the question in this form, in the first place? Surely the central question is about God and not about Jesus Christ. It is. And yet the question about God is not truly faced unless the implication of Jesus Christ for that question is reckoned with. "No man has ever seen God; the only Son, who is in the bosom of the Father, he has made him known." (John 1:18) Man, through the ages, has been incurably religious. He has always known that he was a related creature and, therefore, has constantly sought to define that relatedness. "God" was the term he used to designate this relation; seeking incessantly to find out what God was like and to establish the right relation with Him.

69

All religions bear witness to this quest of man, and all of them carry evidence both of the success of that quest as well as of its failure. For while "God never left himself without witness" (Acts 14:17), the very pervasiveness of that witness made it both inevitable and possible for men to fashion God according to their own imagination. (Acts 17:29)

It is this situation which came to an end with Jesus Christ. Before Him, were "the times of ignorance"; now had come the time of decision. (Acts 17:30) God has been made known, certainly not in Himself, but in His relatedness. He has made himself known as Father through the Son, so that through that same Son, each man and all men may know God as Father. To choose Jesus Christ is to choose to live by this relation in the fullness of its meaning.

It is certainly true that there is a connection between man's religious experience before Jesus Christ and the experience of God in Jesus Christ, but the logic of this connection, whether in the religious history of man or in the religious experience of any particular man, lies in an act of repentance. As Paul puts it, "The times of ignorance God overlooked, but now he commands all men everywhere to repent." (Acts 17:30) Only by this repentance can men reclaim the experience of God which they had before their confrontation with Jesus Christ and make that experience part of their obedience to Him. The choice of Jesus Christ, then, is the decisive issue; and it is this issue with which we shall deal in this chapter.

THE PRICE

However, even before we do that, if we are to do it convincingly, we must make clear an underlying fact which belongs to the nature of all choices—the fact that all choices have to be paid for—and, therefore, the fact that inherent in every choice is a decision concerning the price to be paid and the mode of its payment. Jesus put the matter simply when He said:

> "For which of you, desiring to build a tower, does not first sit down and count the cost whether he has enough to complete it? Otherwise, when he has laid a foundation and is not able to finish, all who see it began to mock him saying, this man began to build and was not able to finish." (Lk. 14:28)

Mark Twain, the creator of Tom Sawyer, makes Tom's friend Huckleberry Finn say: "Well then, what's the use of learning to do right, when it's so troublesome to do right and ain't no trouble to do wrong." But is this true? If God rules the world, then ultimately the world must be obedient to God's character; which means that it is at least as much trouble to do wrong as to do right. God's law holds, the law which says—take what you choose and pay for it. Indeed, whatever you choose, there is no escaping payment.

Then, why is it that we tend to make this mistake of thinking that "it ain't no trouble to do wrong?"—that we do not have to pay? It is because the devil is prepared to allow us credit. If we choose evil, if we choose the worse, the cheaper, we can get what we want at once—and pay later in instalments. Do we want idleness and pleasure?—we can have them at once. We can waste our time, and indulge ourselves immediately. We can get our desire now—but we have to pay later. We pay with a lax character, poor work, ineffective career, and perhaps even more. The devil allows credit but God demands payment in advance. If we choose instead, Christian character, integrity, or even a successful career, we must pay in advance with diligence, hard work, self-control, self-denial, and discipline. It is only when we have paid these that our aim can be effectual. The Christian life is the soldier's life. Victory is at the end of a hard, long fight. Payment now, the reward afterwards. The soldier's song is a true song—"It's a long, long way to Tipperary." But the price is worth the paying—"for my heart is right there."

A little girl was taken to hear a famous Negro singer's rendering of a religious oratorio. The singer had a wonderful voice, and such perfect control that the little girl was enraptured. After the performance, the girl was taken to meet the singer, and cried ecstatically, "I wish I could sing like that!" "Do you?" said the singer. "It took me six hours of practice every day for fifteen years." That was the price she had to pay in advance for the gift of song. But if the highest and noblest is costly, it still does not cost as much as the other. For the other is literally, the devil to pay! It is the devil who sends the bills in, and it is hard enough for the individual to pay; but the devil is not content with that. He sends the bills to those we love, our parents, our families, those we live with, our community, even our nation and the whole world. So that the choice in the last analysis is not between self-sacrifice and self-indulgence; but between two kinds of self-sacrifice.

There is no alternative to self-sacrifice. We have to give ourselves away to someone else. The only question is to whom and when. Should we decide to give ourselves away to God, we must do it immediately; but, if to the devil, then we can do it later and even in instalments.

Take what you choose—take it and pay for it! We desire Christian homes, faithful marriages, the religious and pious training of children. We know that these things are the things we want. But are we prepared to pay the price in advance? Do we not often neglect our daily self-discipline? How often our devotion and prayer time is crowded out of the twenty-four hours, and when opportunities of work and leadership in the church come around, we evade responsibility; we always have an excuse of having too much to do already. Our favourite hypocrisy is to choose the best and decline to pay for it—to pay for it now, for now is the only time when payment can be made. Now is the day of salvation—"today if you should hear his voice harden not your hearts." "Today when it is still today—repent." (Heb. 3:15)

To choose the good and refuse to pay for it involves the choice of the worse—the road to Hell is paved with good intentions and right choices; and he who refuses to pay for the good pays for the worse as the devil sends in his bills; now in deformed character and maimed career—and later in souls that are lost—which is the final payment that the devil demands.

In other words, put directly, there is an alternative to choosing Jesus Christ: only, it is not an alternative choice in the true sense of the word. When Jesus said, "He that is not with me is against me" (Matt. 12:30), this was what He was referring to. The alternative to being for Jesus is to be against Him. It is eventually a choice for or against Him, not a choice between Him and someone else. (There is another verse in Scripture where Christ says, "He that is not against us is for us" (Mk. 9:40), but here the object of choice is not Jesus Christ but the Christian community. Where Jesus Christ is concerned—He that is not with me is against me. Where the Christian community is concerned— He that is not against us is with us.

THE WAY

So we arrive at the final question, the question with which we began,—How is the choice of Jesus Christ made? What does it mean to choose Him? At some point, everyone who is a witness for Jesus Christ will have to face this question. Someone will ask, "Tell me how to meet Jesus, this person who you say is anxious to meet me."

How do we meet a person we have not met before? If I should go to the railway station to meet someone, I must have some idea about the person I have gone to meet or else I shall miss him even if he should be there. Jesus Christ has been there for a long time and we have not met him only because we have missed Him. We do not know enough about Him to recognize Him. Some years ago, I was travelling in the same steamship cabin with a graduate student from the Ceylon University who was going to do postgraduate work at Oxford. More than once, in the cabin, I heard him say to another fellow passenger, "I do not believe that," whenever some subject connected with the Christian faith was raised. One day when he made this remark to me, I said, "Hold on a minute till I get a piece of paper and a pencil and let me write down a list of all the things you do not believe." Before very long I had compiled an imposing list. He did not believe that Jesus Christ was God become

man. He did not believe that Jesus Christ worked any miracles. He did not believe that Jesus Christ died for our sins.
He did not believe that Jesus Christ rose from the dead and so
on. When I had written all this down, I asked him, "When
did you last read any of the gospels?" He looked at me for a
moment and said "Not since I left Sunday School," whereupon I tore into two the paper on which I had written down
his list of unbeliefs and threw it into the wastepaper basket
with the comment that he was intellectually dishonest. He
was pretending unbelief without taking the trouble even to
read the record in which the things he did not believe were
spoken of. There is no cure for second-hand doubt. We can
disbelieve if we want to, but at least we must be honest. It
is not possible to meet Jesus Christ unless we acquaint ourselves again and again with the gospel story which alone can
help us to recognize Him when we meet him.

Secondly, we must ask: are there others who have met
Him and who can describe Him to us? There are men and
women of every age, these last 2000 years, and of every
country who say that they have met Him and can describe
Him. In the realm of Christian literature there is a growing
library of Christian biographies which are nothing more
than laboratory records. These people have lived in a certain way and have as a result made certain discoveries.
Nobody would claim to be a scientist who did not acquaint
himself with the written records of what other scientists had
discovered. And yet there is so little willingness on the part
of many to read Christian biography.

But above and beyond this preparation to recognize Him
when one meets Him is the necessity of wanting to meet

Him. Jesus Christ is not available for casual acquaintance. When, at His trial, Pilate the governor asked Him "What is truth?" Jesus gave no reply. (John 18:38) Pilate was asking Him a rhetorical question, though with some curiosity, and Jesus was silent. If we are to meet Jesus there must be in our attitude more than curiosity. We must want Him.

And then we shall meet Him. I can say no more than that. There are some experiences which are self-validating. When a person is in love he knows he is in love. If he does not know, he is not in love. When we meet Jesus we shall know. I can think of people saying, "Now you are talking about the leap of faith." I am. Gipsy Smith once told a story of picking up his little boy and setting him on a large table. He then stood about a yard from the table and said to his son," Come, jump." The little fellow walked gingerly to the edge of the table, looked at his father, looked at the gap between the table and where the father was standing and then quietly went back and sat in the center of the table. The father stood him up again and said, "Come, jump." This time he stood up at the center of the table, closed his eyes and ran across the table into his father's arms. It was the leap of faith—not a leap out of reason, but a leap into love.

THE RESULT

And when this leap has been made, when the decision has been taken to trust Jesus Christ, when the choice of Jesus Christ has been backed by the willingness to pay the price of discipleship, then and only then do we get answers to many of the questions that we ask in vain before this obedience is given. Why does Christian witness insist on the choice of God in Jesus Christ? Is not God one, so that whatever the name be by which God is called, all are worshiping but the one God? Is not the acceptance of Jesus Christ as a Teacher and Exemplar enough to help one to live the good life? So the questions can be multiplied; but, in the last analysis, the answers come only when Jesus Christ gives the answers himself, and which He does through the life of discipleship alone. To trust Him for the answers is part of the trust we place in Him when we choose Him as our Lord.

One thing more needs to be said—it is that this choice for or against Jesus Christ corresponds also to something in man's very nature. When men choose Him, they find themselves too. The saying of St. Augustine is well known—"Thou hast made us for thyself and we are restless till we find our rest in Thee." This nostalgia is built into us. It is what prompts us to say, "I will arise and go to my father." However, the choice we are talking about is not only a choice to go back to Him, it is a choice to go forward to Him too. God is home as well as the land of promise, so that nostalgia is only one side of man's nature. The other side is the constant striving of man towards a future, his dreams of a world to be. "There is a long, long trail awinding into the land of my dreams." Thus does the challenge to choose for or against Jesus fulfil man himself, answering both his homesickness and also his wanderlust, meeting as much his need for shelter as for adventure. Jesus is the key of the human lock.

"Keep your eyes on the price—hold on,
walk together children—don't get weary."

So go the words of the old Negro spiritual, or, as the modern one puts it,

> "We shall overcome, we shall overcome,
> Someday—I do believe within my heart
> we shall overcome."

But it is not just some day. "Now" is both the day of salvation and of promise, even as the promise is that it is our home which is also our land of inheritance and that this home will come to us. "I saw the new Jerusalem coming down out of heaven." (Rev. 3:12, 21:2)

The Call

In this last chapter, let us, who are called to be His witnesses, consider our own relationship to Jesus. The point we shall try to make is Jesus' concern for us as individuals as distinct from His concern for the work we do for Him. Jesus does call us to the life and work of witness, but within this call we must recognize that it is not so much our service as us whom He wants.

No one served Jesus more than Paul. And therefore a study of Paul and of Jesus' dealings with him will enable us to see this primacy of Jesus' concern for us in a concrete way. Where this primacy is not acknowledged, the connection between the inner secret of the Christian life and its outer expression in Christian witness is severed. When this happens, while ostensibly the work of witness may go on, that work ceases to carry with it the imprint of true Christian living.

CALLED TO BE A SAINT

When on that day on the Damascus road Jesus called Paul, whom did He want? Was it Paul himself, the man; or was it primarily Paul the potential missionary? It is true that Jesus called Paul to be an apostle, but at the same time is it not clear that, but for this call, Paul would never have become a saint? Apostleship was Christ's method with Paul. That at least is how it seems to me.

For Jesus, Paul was not just a means to an end, great though the work was which He accomplished through him. Jesus was primarily concerned with Paul himself. Let us look a little more closely at Paul—his character, his call, his work—in the hope that in us too, whatever our calling in Jesus, there may be born this overmastering sense of Jesus' concern for us. "He loved me and gave Himself for me," (Gal. 2:20) and it is me whom He wants.

What would Paul have been if not for the call of Jesus? A Hebrew of the Hebrews, a Pharisee among Pharisees, of the tribe of Benjamin, of the school of Gamaliel; zealous in an exclusive faith, with the pride of a man who had apprehended and the confidence of a man who was accepted by his own people and honored by the wise in every land. Let us contrast this picture with Paul as he reveals himself in his letters. A man not having yet apprehended, foolish, not knowing anything except the cross, weak and humble for the sake of the gospel, accounted outcast. (Phil. 3:5-6, 14) "We have become," he says, "and are now, as the refuse of the world, the offscouring of all things." (1 Cor 4:13) This contrast is no mere imagination. We can, in fact, trace the conflicts between Paul as he would have been and Paul

as he schooled himself to become, through the pages of the
Acts of the Apostles and in his letters.

Think of Paul, for instance, standing on the Areopagus,
quoting from the poets of Athens; and picture the same
Paul again, as he is in Corinth, preaching the Crucified in
foolishness of words, for he was determined when among
them to be utterly ignorant of everything except of Jesus
Christ. (Acts 17:22, 1 Cor. 2:2)

Or, think again of Paul before Festus, making his appeal
to Caesar. No want of dignity here, no mere acquiescence
now in being regarded merely as an outcast, not willing in
this instance to be treated as anything or anybody. Paul the
Roman citizen speaks and it is with a ring in his voice that
those words are heard: "I stand before Caesar's judgment
seat. I appeal unto Caesar." (Acts 25:11)

Or, let us think again of some of the statements of Paul,
those lightning flashes that we have in his letters which il-
lumine for us the face of the man, and then say what Paul
would have been had not he been called to be an apostle,
had not the Christ crossed his path on the Damascus road.
"We endure anything," he says, "rather than put an obsta-
cle in the way of the gospel of Christ." (1 Cor. 9:12): or,
as he writes in another place, "I am content with weak-
nesses, insults, hardships, persecutions, and calamities: for
when I am weak, then am I strong." (2 Cor. 12:10) Or
hear him again as he says to the Corinthians: "For though I
am free from all men, I have made myself a slave to all, that
I might win the more." (1 Cor. 9:19)

These are not mere flourishes either of speech or of writing. Paul's heart throbs to the music of freedom, his spirit
responds to the idea of strength; and yet he became as a

slave and a weakling because of the calling of God in Jesus Christ. If not for the gospel, he would have been independent, free: binding others perhaps, but not himself being bound. It is to the call of Jesus that we owe the picture of an old man in chains, bond-servant to all. The opposing colors blend, and every time it is for the gospel's sake that the opposite is also true. Independent, and yet for the gospel's sake not free. Strong, and yet for the gospel's sake made weak. Proud, and yet for the gospel's sake humble. Learned, and yet for the gospel's sake accounted a fool.

Leave out the gospel, forget that Paul was called to preach it, and you leave out the saint. Paul owed what he was to the gospel; because of it he attained to a rounded life, a wholeness of personality. Christ had called him—to become an apostle?—yes; but if we must answer the question, "What did the call achieve in Paul during the course of a life-time?" we must say that Christ had called him to become a saint.

CALLED TO BE A MISSIONARY

We have been thinking of Paul and the difference "the call" meant to him as a man. There is a further meaning to be gained by a consideration of his work itself and the way it came to be done, which would help to focus for us the truth we are seeking to understand. Paul was a missionary. He had been called to be an apostle, and it was Paul's ambition and aim to evangelize Asia, push on to Rome, and if possible, get as far as Spain. "I press on," is a phrase that is characteristic of the man. We know also that the preaching of the gospel is God's concern too. He wants it preached and preached to all men everywhere; and yet the Acts of the Apostles tells us that Paul was disappointed at the beginning in both his ambitions. The Council of Jerusalem was over, the charter of Gentile liberty was won, and Paul was on the high road again. Now was the time to evangelize Asia, and then he would be free to push on to Rome; and yet when he attempts to do it at this his first opportunity, he is forbidden—"forbidden by the Holy Spirit." (Acts 16:6) And, as for his second ambition—"Rome"—he did get there, and yet when God sent him there, He sent him in chains.

Of course it was true that all this worked out ultimately towards the furtherance of the gospel. It was possible for Paul, when he was finally permitted to go to Asia, to have the co-operation of Aquila and Priscilla; and as for his bonds, "they became known throughout the whole Praetorian guard." (Phil. 1:13) But what is significant is that God crossed Paul's plans as a missionary, and if the things which happened to Paul fell out rather unto the progress of the gospel, it was also true that they fell out unto the making of Paul as well. The very way in which Paul mentions it shows that he did have his doubts about the plans that God was almost forcing him to follow. In any case, he had been worried. But Paul surrendered, and God's plans proved best both for the work and for the man.

That is what I wish we would remember. Our plans for our work sometimes miscarry and are very often thwarted, and it seems as if the devil has won. Nevertheless, the times are not a few when the truth is neither the one nor the other, but simply this, that God has overruled. And we are called upon to do what Paul had to do, surrender to God's plans; and that not simply because His plans are the best for

His work, but also, if not primarily, because surrender is the best thing for us. It is us God is concerned with.

Paul had his thorn in the flesh and we will have ours, but as for Paul so for us, the only reply to prayer will often be: "My grace is sufficient for you." (2 Cor. 12:9) Did not this thorn hinder Paul in his work? Was it a sickness, or an infirmity? We do not know; but one thing is clear—whatever that thorn might have meant to the work, it was good for Paul in God's sight, and it was Paul whom God was dealing with, Paul whom He wanted.

What about the work then? The question is legitimate and perhaps, in attempting to trace the effect of the call on the life of Paul, we have created an antithesis between the man and his work which is not altogether true. Yet one needs to remember that even if there is no antithesis, there is at least a difference. If God called us, He wants us ourselves; and if we have also been called to work for Him, it is still us He wants; for the demand is not that we work as mere instruments in His hands, but that as sons in His household we share His thoughts and His plans. The synthesis of these two aspects of the call was perfectly realized in Paul. In his case we have the saint and the missionary par excellence—saint through being called to be a missionary, missionary because he was a saint.

We too have been called. How far then is this synthesis true of us? To what extent and with how much confidence can we assert with Paul and say, "We have the mind of Christ," (1 Cor. 2:16) It is a tremendous claim to make, and yet it is the only valid credential of anyone who claims to be "called." If the call means anything it means that. To be called is to achieve in oneself a synthesis between sonship and service; to have the mind of Christ, as a son; to serve with the mind of Christ, as an apostle. We may preach the gospel with our every breath, we may serve our fellows with all our strength and yet what a dangerous possibility Paul pictures when he says, "lest after preaching to others I myself should be disqualified." (1 Cor. 9:27) Yes, it is possible; for the call of Jesus is not merely a call to work, it is a call for me.

"Not that I have already obtained this or am already perfect; but I press on to make it my own, because Christ Jesus has to make me his own." (Phil. 3:12)

Postscript

Why this particular postscript? Because a consideration of the meaning and responsibility of Christian witness cannot be silent on the succession of that witness as it takes place in the home. The implications of this for young people as they choose their life partners, as they marry and build their homes, as they bear and rear children are only too obvious. The purpose of this postscript is to draw attention to what this succession in the home can mean and what it may degenerate into.

Rehoboam begat Abijah: a bad father begat a bad son. Abijah begat Asa: a bad father begat a good son. Asa begat Jehoshaphat: a good father begat a good son. Jehoshaphat begat Jehoram: a good father begat a bad son. (1 Kings 12-22) Let us look at this succession in terms of human responsibility without taking into consideration the infinite possibilities of divine grace, and let it teach us what the responsibilities of parenthood are and what they involve.

Rehoboam begat Abijah. It is but natural that a bad father should have a bad son. It is more than likely that a child will be like his father. It is more correct to say that a child will be like his parents. My son will not only do what I do, but he will be in public what I am in private. I have been the headmaster of a school. Sometimes, teachers have complained about the impertinence of students. Practically always when I inquired into an incident, I found that the impertinence of the boy to his teacher was the consequence of the way in which that teacher had been discussed in the boy's home. When a child finds that its parents do not respect somebody, the child will show this disrespect publicly. This is the kind of experience in which one sees a particular fulfillment of the words of the Master, "Nothing is covered up that will not be revealed, or hidden that will not be known." (Matt. 10:26)

How often parents make the mistake of thinking that they can teach their children to do what they themselves do not do. Parents who never attend public worship send their children to Sunday School. This period of attending Sunday School and church comes to an end with confirmation. Then the children just fall off. They begin to do what their parents used to do. A friend of mine who is doing very well in life said to me one day concerning his son, "I am giving him a good education. I can get him into a good employment. I shall leave him a sizable inheritance. But all this is useless, if I fail to teach him the fear and love of God." How true this is! But how is this to be accomplished? There is ample warning in the simple sequence that a bad father begets a bad son.

But Abijah begat Asa. A bad father begat a good son. How does this happen? It happens because no man is purely good or purely bad. There is a poem by G. A. Studdert Kennedy addressed to his son Patrick, in which he says:—

"I gave thee life, my little son,
    And thou art part of me;
Which part? would God I knew the Truth,
    Then were my soul set free
From fretting fears all down the years,
    From dull anxiety;

> Lest I have given thee that part,
> Which makes my angel weep,
> That underworld whence lusts and lies,
> Like vermin, crawl and creep
> Across my visions and my prayers;
> Whence selfish passions leap [1]

When my brother obtained his medical degree and became a doctor, my father rejoiced not simply at the success of his son, but in the fact that his son achieved what was his own ambition. My father had wanted to become a doctor but could not because his father did not have the money to give him such an expensive education. So he took to law instead. My brother fulfilled my father's dreams.

Our children see not only what we are, but also sense what we want to be. They have an insight into our striving for goodness, into our struggles with our badness. They inherit both sides of our nature. Our actuality is theirs and also our ideals. So that it is possible, and thank God it is possible, that a bad father can have a good son.

But how often this possibility is not fulfilled because parents manage to hide from their children the agony of their striving and the shame of lost contests. It is perhaps even true of some that they are just bad and there is no striving for goodness at all.

> "All instincts immature
> All purposes unsure,
> All I could never be

[1] *The Unutterable Beauty*, by G. A. Studdert Kennedy, London: Hodder and Stoughton Ltd., 1927.

All men ignored in me.
This, I was worth to God
Whose wheel the pitcher shaped." [2]

Asa begat Jehoshaphat—a good father begat a good son. If it is true that our children have to carry us as part of their lives, it is true not only of parents who are part of a child's handicap but also of parents who are a child's goodly heritage. We live in our children.

When the writer to the Hebrews compares life to a relay race, he speaks of those who have gone before us cheering us on as we run our lap of the race. It is so often the case that the torch we carry is the torch our parents carried before us. We inherit the causes they strove for, the ideals for which they stood, the battles they fought. What a sad thing it is when a parent arrives at the end of his race without the torch, or to change the figure, having dropped the baton. It is a sadder story when parents hand over to their children the grievances they carried and the vendettas they nursed. Of course, some parents have nothing to hand over. They just lived.

We must never think, however, that it is a foregone conclusion that a good father will have a good son. It is said that Jehoshaphat begat Jehoram. Jehoram was a bad son of a good father. How does this happen? It mostly happens when parents do not give time to their children to inherit their goodness. They are so good that they spend all their time outside their home, engaged in doing good to others. Children of such parents grow up deprived of any real knowledge of what their parents are like.

[2] "Rabbi Ben Ezra," by Robert Browning.

As I write this, I think of a home I know where the parents are lovely people but the children are wayward and indisciplined. Any true discipline of children must be based, not simply on the nature of the deed done but on the nature of the child. But how will parents know their child, unless they live with that child and observe him grow and give him companionship along the way. The idea that children can be helped simply by a good example is a false one. Children know too much of their parents to accept their good example at face value.

Studdert Kennedy has also written a poem addressed to his second son, Christopher. He says:

> Bear Thou the Christ,
> My little son.
> He will not burden Thee,
> That Holy One.
> For, by a mystery,
> Who beareth Him He bears
> Eternally,
> Up to the radiant heights
> Where Angels be,
> And heaven's crimson crown of lights
> Flames round the crystal sea.[3]

The parents' task is to make every child a Christopher, a bearer of Christ. Then alone is the task accomplished.

[3] *The Unutterable Beauty*, by G. A. Studdert Kennedy.

Discussion Questions

"THE ISSUE"

1. How realistic is the conversation of this chapter? Do you know anyone who talks or thinks this way? Do *you* think or talk this way?
2. Which of the characters of the chapter sounds most like you? Why?
3. Why is it difficult "to talk about Jesus and ourselves at the same time"?
4. Are you aware of the active presence of Christ with you? What helps make His presence real for you? What hinders this?
5. Give your understanding of the sentence: "The resurrection keeps tearing holes."

"THE EVENT"

1. Which of the four explanations of "God as my Portion" is most meaningful to you? Why?
2. What do you think it means in concrete terms to have "joy from an event that has happened to us—the event of having been claimed for the gospel and of having claimed the gospel"?
3. Discuss: "She had lost her faith in Him, but she had not lost Him. He remained. He always remains."
4. In what sense can *you* say Jesus Christ has "become part of your life"?
5. What are the implications for this particular day in your life of what Dr. Niles calls "the necessity to see others in Jesus Christ and to see Jesus Christ in others"?

"THE CHOICE"

1. How do you describe to others what it means for you "to believe"?
2. Which of the five dimensions of "believing" described by Dr. Niles relates best to people today? Do you think any of them is especially suited to young people? Why?
3. Do you consider "the notion of faith" radical? Why?
4. What does it mean to speak of the "secular quality of the Christ-event"? Does this "exert pressure on the human will and the human mind" as Dr. Niles says? Why?
5. Identify parallels in your own experience of the gospel pattern for life: a borrowed manager; the public street; an upper room; a lonely garden; the hill outside the city; an open tomb.

"THE FAMILY"

1. Discuss: "We must live close enough to people so that they can see us as we really are" in the light of today's seemingly constant search for identity.
2. What is Dr. Niles saying as he pinpoints the truth that the petitions of the Lord's Prayer are "petitions in the plural"? Why?
3. Does it make any difference to you to say "Our Father" and have the "our" mean the Christian family or the whole human family? Explain.
4. Do you think most people include "the whole world economy" in the Lord's Prayer petition for daily bread? Do you?
5. What does Dr. Niles mean by "the meaning and scope of our common life"? *Whose* common life does he mean? Why does he devote a whole chapter to this?

6. Discuss: "There is an equal place for not talking about Jesus, for just getting on with the job in hand."

"THE ADVENTURE"

1. Evaluate Dr. Niles' threefold impact of the gospel. Is this an adequate description of "conversion"? Do the three parts ever happen simultaneously? Explain.
2. What limitations can you think of being caused by using the word "servant" in a contemporary discussion of the witnessing life? Are these insurmountable? What word would you use?
3. Discuss: "Faithful evangelism will not necessarily win acceptance."
4. What are the practical implications of having "concern for people as people?"
5. Give your understanding of St. Vincent de Paul's words: "Love them, they will then forgive you your charity."

"THE ALTERNATIVE"

1. Do most people think "it ain't no trouble to do wrong?" Why?
2. Discuss: "The devil allows credit but God demands payment in advance."
3. Dr. Niles believes "it is eventually a choice for or against Him (Christ), not a choice between Him and someone else." What's the difference between Christian particularity and bigotry or intolerance?
4. Dr. Niles says man has always known he is a related creature and has constantly sought to define that relatedness. Evaluate some modern meanings of "relationship" in view of this search.

5. What has been the price to you for the choice of Christ? To those around you?

6. Explain: "There is no cure for second-hand doubt."

"THE CALL AND POSTSCRIPT"

1. What do you think—when Jesus called Paul on the Damascus Road, did He want Paul himself, the man, or primarily Paul the potential missionary? Why do you think so?

2. Are you able to "surrender" when God overrules your plans? What about the patriarchs and prophets who argued with God? And Christ's story of the widow who kept coming to the judge (Luke 18:1-8)?

3. What does it mean to "have the mind of Christ?" Do you? How do you know?

4. Is this true: "Our children see not only what we are, but also sense what we want to be?" What difference does it make, one way or the other?

5. When does your "parenthood" begin—at the birth of your first child? At its conception? At your marriage? At your birth? Or?

6. How does Dr. Niles describe the task of parents? Do you agree? Why?